THE RASHOMON SYNDROME

Books by Pamela Gillilan

That Winter (Bloodaxe Books, 1986)
The Turnspit Dog, with Charlotte Cory (Bloodaxe Books, 1993)
All-Steel Traveller: New & Selected Poems (Bloodaxe Books, 1994)
The Rashomon Syndrome (Bloodaxe Books, 1998)

PAMELA GILLILAN

The
Rashomon
Syndrome

BLOODAXE BOOKS

ISBN: 1 85224 465 8

First published 1998 by
Bloodaxe Books Ltd,
P.O. Box 1SN,
Newcastle upon Tyne NE99 1SN.

Bloodaxe Books Ltd acknowledges
the financial assistance of Northern Arts.

Cover printing by J. Thomson Colour Printers Ltd, Glasgow.

Printed in Great Britain by
Cromwell Press Ltd, Trowbridge, Wiltshire.

Let a man get up and say, 'Behold this is the truth', and instantly I perceive a sandy cat filching a piece of fish in the background. Look, you have forgotten the cat, I say.

VIRGINIA WOOLF

It is all very well to copy what you see, but it is much better to draw only what you still see in the memory. This is a transformation in which imagination collaborates with memory. Then you only reproduce what has struck you, that is to say the essential, and so your memories and your fantasy are freed from the tyranny which nature holds over them.

DEGAS, cited in Georges Jeanniot
'Souvenirs sur Degas' in *Révue Universelle*

Syndrome: (Oxford) A concurrence: a set of concurrent things (1646)

Acknowledgements

Acknowledgements are due to the editors of the following publications where some of these poems first appeared: *Outposts, Poetry Wales, The Poet's Voice, Prop* and *Ver Anthology* (Ver Poets, 1997).

Contents

With Subtitles

(Rashomon, dir. Akira Kurosawa, 1950)

Foliage hems the forest path;
through dappled black and white
they make their jubilant way.
She's in pale finery, face secret
beneath a wide brim swathed
in flimsy silk. Her lord, on foot,
leads the fine horse she rides.

Then suddenly there's terror.
A bandit leaps upon them,
stamping strong bare feet,
flailing a fearsome sword.

That's my remembered scene,
the point from which those three
would, each in turn protagonist,
enact divergent stories
of betrayal and dishonour;
the point of questioning.

Did the man guard his wife
or did he run, save himself?
Do I see him shamed, bare-breasted,
self-stabbed at the clearing's edge?
Did she struggle, fight the villain off
or welcome, almost, a rough violation?

Only the theme seems certain –
one watcher's tale is not another's
though they stood together in the street,
heard the same scream of brakes.
My brother's mother is mine also
but from childhood years we've stored
insular memories, diversely lit,
of her and of incident and circumstance.
But it wasn't like that, we cry, each
defending an unshakeable recall
of a shared past event.

Advancement, Tudor Style

(Henry VIII at Stratford, February 1997)

Ambition's the flail
that keeps the field running.
Fences, blind leaps, pitfalls,
briars, brooks and brakes,
snares sprung underfoot –
all must be overcome.

With each gain new handicaps pile on –
hindrance of fur and velvet,
heaviness of gold,
chainweight of obligation:
but nothing, not even fear,
halts the forward rush.

Have you a fox's cunning? Can you crawl
beneath and around like a viper,
swoop like a hawk, adopt new colours
like a chameleon? Can you jostle and elbow,
trip up and outstrip? Arrived,
can you hold your place? But maybe

you're not ambitious for a brow
shadowed with scarlet or circled
with marks of rank? It's wiser, then,
to run in a minor league, or to jog on
less cumbered, less remarked,
amongst the bunched mid-field.

Eminence has its price. Anne Bullen
went cheerfully to the scaffold,
to the sword-stroke's clean release
from years of nights bestraddled
by a diseased and mountainous lord,
and never a safe moment.

A Firm Persuasion

Two lots of banns read – what was he about,
hedging his bets, playing two girls along
to matrimony's brink? He was found out,
of course. Whether his Anne was wrong
or right for him or would have been first choice
we can't guess, since her father clinched the match
with hard cash and authoritative voice.
He'd have had no idea the kind of catch
young Will would prove but, soon to bear a child,
Anne wanted wifehood; and perhaps Will gained
some steadiness from her, became less wild.
But that small cottage, thatched and many-paned,
was not enough. He flew the pretty cage
for roistering company, the magnet stage.

Bank Robbery

She's dead, they said, gently
raising her bonneted head
from the timber sidewalk –
shot blind through a door.
In the wrong place
at a dangerous time she'd tried
the bank door handle.

Well, I thought, she'd have been dead
anyway by now if she'd been a real
long-skirted nice young woman,
raising her child in a dry western land
a century ago, and not an actress
with a small part in a movie.

I'd been too late for the beginning
but I watched until the finish.
The horses were magnificent,
thundering across vast scenery,
glossy-coated in spite of the dust
but I tired of the shooting –

the wheee and wham of bullets;
and the corpses – a score or so of men
but only the one woman – a lost life
for which I admit I shed a tear
because of the unwittingness
of her hand on the door.

Chop!

there's an ear gone
a hand lopped
from a casbah thief

bough dropped by the axe
hair torn from a head
in extreme of grief.

Chop! it's the last
chop – a heart stopped
drowned in its own flow

no purpose or passion
just that past hopes now
are cropped too soon.

Chop! the unseen
gene that stopped
your mother's breath

early has snapped your thread –
all your life it has been
working to set the hour

of your death   in the dead
hour of the night
your death.

The Bequest

Rosenthal, a friend said, holding a cup
against daylight, putting irrelevant title
to celebration's shape – white white,
nature-bright clusters, plum and peach –
the best set brought out for birthdays,
Christmas, Easter, the visitored sunlit
Sunday teas of Spring.

Afternoon ceremony confirmed my mother's role.
No child or challenger handled the cosied pot.
The fruited jugs and bowl by her right hand
stood on a galleried tray of milky glass
haunted subsurface by pale grapes –
lilac-grey printed shadows.

The tea-set's mine now, stored
in the dark sideboard, plates and saucers
embraced and sandwiched in clean paper,
two steady stacks with no uncovered chink.
Singly-wrapped cups stand coupled one in one;
not, so far, used by me – their emptiness
too full to hold more tea.

Coming Round

He was still a bit dopey
but cheerful. 'I'm fine.
Soon be back on form,
kicking the ball around.
I'm told the car's a write-off.
Yes, there is a thing
you can do for me –
that extra blanket.
My legs feel so cold.'

Across the foot-end
of the hospital bed
she spread the doubled blanket.
It lay flat as a board.

'Thanks,' he said,
'Sure to warm up soon.'

For Lauren

I recall our first meeting;
she sat at my daughter's table –
a slight girl in tight leathers.

Who'd have guessed nothing would last
for her – the turncoat partners,
the fears and partings,

her invaded body's losing fight?
It was a heart from a dead young man
that failed beneath her healed ribs.

There would have been a second chance;
but she made a will – thoughts
for her small children's care.

Resolved, resigned,
she turned a wintered face from the world,
her scant dole of days consumed.

Poppy

Kiss me, she says, and for perhaps
the fourth time in our lives
our lips meet, hers narrowed and dry.
She's propped against spotless pillows
like a prammed and cherished baby –

forthright and leaderly woman, now
hardly more than her own ghost,
cheeks tissue-white, dark pupils
like small stones without gloss or sparkle
cupped deep in their bony bowls.

The true distress unvoiceable,
he worries about morphia's hold –
but there's no choice; she welcomes
its embrace, more precious to her soon
than food or drink or lover.

Needlework

(in memory of a cousin)

The frame stands by the sofa's arm.
A pointillisme of wool and silk
half-fills the taut circle.
Something meticulous and delicate
as a bird on a bough, a flower-child with wings,
has been begun.

The window's high, above the flight of gulls;
beyond is the wide sky, the sea,
the weather endlessly conceiving fresh designs;
never finite, never finished.

The needle is looped with thread.
The spread of embroidered colour
stilled against barren canvas
is as untouchable, almost,
as those white clouds drifting by.

Yesterday

We heard sirens, paused in our walk
to look down over the railed height.
Blue flashing lights; the traffic halted –
ambulance, fire engines, a platform
on a long arm angled to reach up
to where a slumped shape lay, small
on the grassed roof of the canopy
that shields the riverside road.
Evening climbers clinging, roped,
to the face of the gorge had seen him
plunge past them from the bridge.
Today, a few newspaper lines; a student...

And this morning on the stone-sharp beach
beneath a Dorset cliff Jenny was found.
I think of their last seconds: he
launching down by intent and she,
walking the high grassy path, alone
in warm midsummer air, a rich moon rising –
betrayed by unknown mischance.

It's said that those who fall surprised
don't suffer the whole drop; shock
punches blood from the heart, stops the breath;
that the spirit leaves at the brink – it's not
a sentient thing that breaks on rocks or water.

Carpe Diem

(Montillou, Dordogne, October 1998)

Sit at a chosen viewpoint
on a riverbank or by a table
heaped with fruit in season.
Consider the balance and poise
of rocks or roofs or apples.

Let eye and mind engage
and the hand obey.
Observe the weight of shadows,
the breadth or narrowness of intervals.

Be aware of the sap rising
through the capillaries of poplars,
and of the transparent strength
of a green glass jug, how its body
received the molten handle.
See how every kind of leaf
grows to its own template.

Remember the tilt of a head,
the impress of a hand,
the words just spoken.
Know that you're here
in this frail moment.
Reach for a brush, a pen.

Juniors

(for J.M.)

A bit of bravado got us together –
my leap off a strawstack, dared by his big sisters.
'That little girl won't be afraid!'
I was only by chance passing the yard gate.

I was eight, he eleven – hair black and straight,
face sallow from east London living,
eyes an ardent brown. I hope you can believe
it was love – I still do. But one threat

soiled that idyllic summer – the farmer's son,
his smile mocking above fingers that slowly
teased from his work-greased waistcoat pocket
a glimpse of pencilled paper. Our love letters.

We'd thought them posted safely, weighted by stones,
wedged in ivied gateposts. 'Don't tell! Please don't.'
He laughed at our dismay, turned our hearts' secrets
over in his hands. Just children's silliness...

A war and two spells of peace have passed.
I'm idling through the London *A to Z*
and – there's the Hackney page. The street
I know he lived in isn't there.

Schoolgirl

(for F.W.)

We got so good at kissing, hours
of it on the front room sofa,
curtains drawn against daylight;

hours in Finchley Coliseum's
dark back row: *I Cover the Waterfront*,
Bolero – we saw part of so many films;

hours, thigh against thigh
with a book on our knees, reading
steadily through H.G. Wells, turning

our lips towards each other between pages.
My mother can't have missed
the swollen redness of my mouth

but she'd say nothing.
Six years my senior, almost family –
of course you could be trusted.

Brading

Tiptoeing down the hall, one of us trod
on the loose floorboard, jolted Grandfather
to a stop at half past two.
What sort of time was that?
she said at breakfast – our friend,
married and housed high
betwen the downs and the sea.

She kept an eye on us, warned us;
showed us the high-jinks laundry
just along the road
where the girls were always
getting pregnant, silly things.

London had offered us no such stories,
nor husbands who fashioned violins,
sang in the church choir,
would soon be twenty-one;
nor sunswept piers where boys
waited to pick us up –
two red-headed sixteen-year-olds
they may have thought ripe for conquest.

Ripe enough; we might have taken home
more than souvenir seaside rock
but for the dire example
of those rash laundry-girls.

August

(for C.S.)

Riding around the lanes
we stopped at dusk by a field gate,
wheeled our bikes through, leant them
against the hawthorn hedge.

The ground was set hard into the ruts
of old rains, but we found
a smoother slope to lie on.
Well, passion might have built

except that, the sky's blue darkening,
we turned to a new brightness growing
along the meadow's edge; and then
the rising of a vast, round, moon.

Town moons had never
been so brilliant, seemed so near,
shed down such ripened light,
nor called out such a crowd.

Whole families ran, scampering
and tumbling across the grass.
Bold in their play they rushed
so close to where we lay

we almost saw each single hair, each
twitching nose, each jet-bead eye,
each sensitive long ear – tonight
oblivious of threat. We watched

until, limbs stiff, we had to move.
Under that sailing lamp
we walked our bikes in silence,
towards our separate beds.

The Swimmer

(for D.B.)

Suppose, on the night of the party
when he bedded me down – sixteen,
high on excitement and wine,
he had not gently put away my hands,
gone, after just an embrace,
to sleep elsewhere in the house.

There were never promises.
We swam and walked together,
lay long in summer thickets
adrift in each other's arms,
kissed in the scented smoky air
of Odeons and Astorias.

I've no photographs
to help me towards his image;
but I have it, the way it was –
the grace of movement, the humour,
the curved mouth that, above all,
fostered that year's adoration.

There was no sudden schism, no hurt;
each on scarcely perceptible tides
turned towards other consummations.

Shame

The girl at number twenty
began to bleed on the tram,
bled in anguish all along the street,
died indoors.

We'd no idea how or why, in those days
before sex on the curriculum
when parents were too shy to tell;
when in suburbia unmarried mothers
never pushed a pram; no public airing
for sin's issue – spirited away,
adopted, or sometimes presented
as its own grandmother's child.

I remember Lyndie, long plaits,
white ankle-socks – she'd met a soldier
on the Downs, and known no better –
hidden, as she grew big, in a home
for fallen girls, set to sew gowns
for virtuous women's babies;
her own, born into poorhouse calico,
held, quickly taken.

Then came public chastening,
abasement before flinty elders,
stiff-suited, buttoned-up, wearing,
as if of right, their righteousness.

Sans Souci

They came in faultless parcels,
strong brown wrapping taut
over the block of tins –
jubilant matt blue
lettered with gold:
a thousand cigarettes.
I remember their soft conformity –
sherbet-white cylinders close-bedded;
the shine of the lifted lid;
the spicey smell.

There was something festive
about each delivery, anticipation
of pleasure in our father's
ritual unwrapping –
no more sense of harm
than when we played with mercury,
magic metal that scattered to pinpoint beads
or ran together, an unscarred whole,
at the touch of our teasing fingers.

The Gates

In Finchley (where I lived when young)
there were more dead than living men,
brought to their rest from nearer Town:
St Pancras, Marylebone, Islington.

Most days we'd see a funeral pass –
black-plumed black horses in the shafts
of pram-sprung coaches, beetle-black.
White faces nodded in the dark –
was it to hide or mimic grief
each pressed a starch-white handerchief
with gloved hand against mouth or eye?
As each slow cavalcade passed by
we'd peer intently, try to pierce
the flash and shadow of the glass,
discern the traces grief might make –
puffed eyelids, tear tracks on a cheek.
No one stared back, or noticed us,
impertinently curious.

Southward, they'd sit with heads less bowed,
clip-clopping down the Great North Road,
the sable horses pulling home.
Sometimes, long box and flowers gone,
a solitary hearse would pass,
a palanquin of polished glass,
returning down the tramline route
to Holloway or Upper Street
past monumental mason's yards
where plinthed among sharp marble shards
angels held wreaths or lily blooms;
where crosses, pillars, smooth headstones
awaited names, dates, R I P,
a craftsman carved identity
and then the setting into place
beyond those gates of iron lace
we gazed through, going to school each day.

The lawns were graced with yew and bay,
vast cedars, evergreen and dark,
and flower-beds bright as any park.
Invitingly the gates stood wide;
we never dared one step inside.

Eye to Eye?

My father liked to philosophise,
to set discussions going.
Ideas – in my almost-adulthood
I'd get quite drunk on them, not able
to sift the unoriginal and homespun
from the great; it was all new and heady.

How do you know, he'd say,
that your colours are the same as mine?
Red, I'd argue, is fierce – fire,
blood, sunrise – and green is calm,
gentle. How could grass glare like poppies,
buttercups bloom emerald or purple?

He painted landscapes, seascapes –
and if the ultramarine I saw
ran claret-dark for him, the hue still served
for both our seas: my blue, his ruby,
crested with unchallenged white, for white
is no colour and all colours.

Is your indigo as deep as mine,
your yellow, coral, flame, cerulean,
as clearly radiant? Does the meadow
in your eyes match the one I see?
Is earth itself trustworthy – ochre,
umber, clay? How does your garden grow?

Saying It Nicely

(E.M. Berens: *Myths and Legends of Greece and Rome,* revised 1892)

This is a book my father owned, art-student
at Goldsmiths in the 1910s – and often,
though pocket-size, it's as informative
as Larousse, but prim – the rapes and lusts
made mild – and as for Priapus...

Son of Dionysus and Aphrodite (so it runs),
Priapus was god of fruitfulness, protector
of flocks, bees, grapes. His statues, honoured
with milk, honey, the first fruits of field and garden,
served also to scare crows, this god's appearance
being especially repulsive.

Carved likenesses of him in wood or stone
were downward from the hips merely rude columns.
He's shown as having a red and ugly face,
holding a pruning knife, and crowned
with a wreath of vine and laurel,
and though fruit may be carried in his garments
or a cornucopia in his hand he always keeps
his singularly revolting aspect.

The prose I drew this from hints cautiously
at Priapus' condition. A rude column... exposed...
His image stands in a small room in Pompeii.
Some people gasp as they go in; but crows,
I think, might well have perched unscared
on that great phallus, as on a living bough.

Me?

(The Annunciation, Filippo Lippi, National Gallery)

The angel is kneeling, it's true,
and no more than an envoy
(high-ranking, though –
fancy collar, epauletted tunic)
but his gesture's admonitory;
she has no choice.
Her face is wax-like –
it's her right hand,
curved towards the midriff,
that mimes wonder.

You, my virgin heart's idol,
strolled up to me at the pool-side.
   I've a couple of tickets...
   Tonight... Would you like...
Before I could catch it back –
    What, me? I said.

Volunteer for Liberty

(for Jeff Mildwater)

Loving, but not quite lovers –
my mind filled with the wherewithal
to pass exams, his a self-culled library
of philosophy and politics – that summer
our companionship was lively with debate.
Suddenly, without word, he went to war.

A band of brothers, unexhorted by any
king-commander, they joined the people's fight
in Spain – not for adventure, or blindly;
they were born of a wounded generation,
knew widowed mothers, stump-limbed fathers
propped to sell matches at the kerb.

He came home with no more than a limp,
a bullet-broken knee, brought me a bracelet
set with mauve stones, transparencies
of amethyst or glass, a trinket made rare
by its bringing out of that injured land.
I wore it then, wore it decades later

when we met again – a cliché – under a station clock.
Had he lived by the comrade fervour of that time,
valued his life the more because of risk
and reprieve, since Death stalking the olive trees
had not beckoned him? He still seemed
courageous enough for battle, if he saw cause.

Volunteer for Liberty was the paper of the 15th International Brigade,
the British brigade that fought in the Spanish Civil War alongside
those of at least twelve other nationalities. The last verse owes
much to a poem of John Lepper's: *'Death stalked the olive trees /
Picking his men. / His leaden finger beckoned / Again and again.'*

Bruce

The playground shapes loomed
grey against grey on a night
tented with cloud. No moonlight
to sharpen detail, to gleam
along metal struts and chains
child-clutched to a polish.

We climbed over the locked gate,
he in his dark Aussie greatcoat,
I in airwoman's blue. Silently
in synchronised arcs we nursed
our disparate childhoods.
Darwin. London.

Soon our swinging slowed.
Feet on slippery grass,
seats pulled towards each other,
cables strained aslant, through
the frame's iron triangle
we kissed, warming our lips.

In that flat land of hangars,
huts and runways he was homesick
and (he was aircrew) scared,
although he'd never say so.
Ours was hardly a romance
and yet from all those years ago

I can remember his thin face
and how he looked down as he talked,
from shyness or reserve. I know
the way he walked, the angle
of his head, his cautious smile;
I can't recall his leaving.

Over to Framlingham

Elms stand at the meadow's edge.
White cloud-columns echo their shape,
building all afternoon
slowly and lazily, until a moment
(it seems unforeseen and sudden)
when hazy August sunlight
sharpens to acid purity.

Each leaf distinct and gleaming,
the trees leap to relief,
new green against a bruised sky
the colour of bramble-stain staled
on old linen, or of the grapes
that hang ripe from the gnarled vine
of the vicar's greenhouse.

Beneath that frowning purple all hues
take on a limelight brilliance –
the garden a painted set,
geraniums, sunflowers, trellised roses,
meticulous and unmoving;
the pantiled roof new-fired vermilion
against the clouds' dark foil.

That'll go, the old man says,
over to Framlingham. And so it does,
the weight of it rolling northward,
raindrops and hailstones pursed.
We watch the lightning, count the seconds
of sound-lag. A few round tokens
bloom on the dry path, and fade; downpour
is over Framlingham.

A Garden

(for John Manning)

There was a place I loved
and a man; he was seventy
and I twelve – and he died.
Now his small plot of land
answers another hand.

Are columbines growing there,
pink roses wide as saucers,
wild-blue lupins, moon daisies
and his favourite yearly-sown
pungent nasturtium flowers?

He went to the churchyard,
lies by the edge where garlic
and white jack-in-the-hedge
flourish beyond the scythe.
No name above his head –

his cross
of oak, not stone,
is gone.

Beyond Illogan

Even in high August old odours
haunted her house
the residues of musty winters
ineradicable in the plaster
compounding the smeech
of blackened oil-lamp wicks,
candlewax, crusted flues.
Everything that gave light or heat
left its smoke or smear or cinder.
All day on the hob
flames, faggot-lit at morning, licked
the iron kettle's soot-furred curve,
teased out fitful singing –
an endless simmering that staled
the water of all virtue.

Are there homes, still, like hers,
unchanged since their night-building
amongst mine-tunnelled hills;
lives like hers, without ornament
or comfort? She would sit in her one
cushionless wood chair beneath a stern
whiskered grandfather
framed on the limewashed wall.
She would bake hard buns,
without saffron, almost currantless,
persuade the milkman to pause and eat
on his thrice-weekly calls
to her roadless valley.

Country Living, 1955

It was different when he played in London.
Now he comes home heavier by pounds,
wet soil impacted into cloth and skin,
face earthed and sweaty. It was different

in London, with a warm plunge after.
The steam smoothed, softened him,
made him shine – that and the post mortem
with mates in the bar. Now he washes

bit by bit in the kitchen, stove-heated water
drawn from the well, laborious pailfuls.
His boots aren't dry all season; dubbiny, soggy,
they wait out each week until Saturday's

emergence, the brushing away of mildew's frosting.
He laces them on, after socks and pads and socks,
and clatters up the village hill in kit
that still smells of effort and wormcasts.

I prepare, as if awaiting a midwife,
the bowls of hot water that will wash him
incompletely clean – though cleaner than I,
in the guilt of my grudging. For him

the afternoon escape to air and speed;
dull indoor tasks for me. The black
reluctant coalstove glowers, the baby's
wrapped hunger simmers in the pram

and I have too little trust or clarity,
struggling against the moment's bonds,
though of themselves they'll fall; and he,
whom indeed I love, won't make old bones.

The Butler's House

(a season at Heligan)

A hooded friar had been seen to crouch
by the room's darkest wall; incense
and incantation drove him home.

It was our year of fallow living.
We laid our mattress on the boarded floor,
slept well in thick-walled sanctuary.

Tides of foliage lapped against the house.
Beneath rhododendrons' adamant green domes
the native, gentler, spread succumbed.

Trees, dizzy columns, lifted to the light.
We gathered fallen branches for our fires,
lugged oil and water home in cans and pails.

At night, the lamps in golden tongue,
there was no silence, always the taunt
of subliminal speech or song,

the woods' night-voices, part wind, rustle
and sway, part ghost. The people had long gone,
the big-house people, all who served them.

Once the passage of high-wheeled traps
pursuing their year-round errands
had kept the estate roads clear. Now

only rutted ways through arching boughs,
encumbering brambles, led up to the lapsed,
green-veiled, sequestered gardens.

Scars

Live in a town a long time
and you don't forget the wounds –
the footings of a pillared shop gone down
beneath the high stools of a coffee bar;
the new chemists' dustless aisles
haunted by echoing stone arches –
the vanished market hall, its granite,
iron, slate, thrown down and carted off.

The family main-street drapers' is new-risen –
clear light and carpeted open-plan,
the season's short-lived fashions
racked to tempt on chromium carousels
where once in dim upstair fitting-rooms
farmers' wives peered into venerable mirrors
choosing best coats and hats for market days.
Across the ceiling, wooden shuttles stuffed
with pound notes, shillings, pence, were sped
by wire and pulley to the cashier's pulpit –
payment on the dot, or in unhurried settlement
of penned bills dated Michaelmas or Lady Day.
Above long panelled counters, thick mahogany,
hung brass rods like trapezes, carriers
for scarves and printed tea-cloths flatly draped,
sampled from stock behind the scenes.
That warren of departments, the deep drawers,
the shelves of ancient-labelled cardboard boxes,
the lino floors and balustraded stairs,
made a vast, leaping, bonfire.
Not a spool of thread or a child's sock
was saved; swirled down the drain the ash
of haberdashery and underwear.

Almost as suddenly as fire, bulldozers
made their sweep. Revealed by a widened road
a gable line on a once-inner wall recalls
the butcher in his shop. Heavy, hawk-nosed.
he would stomp stiffly between hook and block,
steel on a strap bumping his apron.

Next-door's elegant façade, its stone steps
and pedimented porch, was felled too,
only a memory left.

There are scars older than these – and newer.
My own hurt heals. I can stand alone now,
released at last to go anywhere –
the house, the town, receding into time
but never wholly absent.

Slave Port

Fetter, manacle,
chain, collar,
shackles pegged to stone.

Would you like to have a look?
The visitor declines politely,
edges past a locked door
fronting downward steps
to the cellar's earthy floor,
its rusted cold remains
of iron restraint.

How many of this city's bland façades
conceal such relics of old shame –
dank vaults where living cargo lay
awaiting forward shipment?
Each batch a petty merchant's stock,
a bit of a flutter.

Upstairs, dinner served on porcelain,
families settling between smooth sheets,
their prayers said – all the good wives,
the children, the servants
who speak when they're spoken to.

What the eye doesn't see...
Ask no questions...

Chopsticks

When they dine at *The Sultan of the North*
she eats chicken korma – the mildest dish
among the list of fierce flavours;
and the drinks are soft, flower-scented,
delicately effervescent.

But at *Golden Lotus* – they've met
at the railway station, kissed, walked
arm in arm and fingers interlaced to this
so-peaceful restaurant and been served
gins and tonic while they think about it –
she could enjoy anything from the menu
but chooses chicken again,
with mushrooms and pecans,
and he fancies something sweet-and-sour
and proves himself deft with chopsticks
unfalteringly lifting rice grains
and morsels of spicy meat to his lips.

But, seeing no need to practise
precarious oriental skills, she takes a spoon –
first-learned, still simplest way
of bringing food from bowl to mouth.

Their Song

(Regent Street, Clifton)

Walking out, I passed two fellas
rolling full beer-kegs, to stack
then slide through trapdoors folded back
revealing under-sidewalk cellars.
From each man-handled weight
low rumblings reached the street.

Walking home I saw the men
now hardly stooping to the task –
a light push and each cask
towards the kerb-edge spun.
Bang, rattle, crash and thrum...
each jostling barrel-drum
rang like a tuneless gong –
their vacancy their song.

A Glass of Sherry

(Bristol: Park Street to Clifton Village)

Fat woman runs penguin-footed
to catch a bus. Unsilenced motorbike
snarls uphill. Two bow-tied young men:
each holds a shallow box on forearms,
fingers hinged from upturned palms.
They pass close, the chink
of glass on glass just audible
like pinpoint chirpings
from the smallest chicks imaginable.

A number eight swings to the kerb,
empty. Good as a taxi.

A Dynarod van's an impossible vermilion.
The lion's pure gold, the unicorn white
(of course) on the Gallery portico.
Magnolia flowers not proof against the wet
are bearing this dry blustery wind.
Conifers slimmer than cypresses
stand in a rank of three – so vertical
they might be strung from their tips
taut-lined to sky-hooks.

Forsythia in the Square's garden
is thick-custard yellow.
My window-box daffodils are dry tissue
ravelled on apologetic stems.
I can't think what should be next.
Lobelia? Busy Lizzie? I need tea.
Even a small glass of sherry
heightens the senses unduly, taken
without food, mid afternoon.

The Tripod Horse

(Symondsbury, Dorset, New Year 1998)

It's rained all day, though now the stars are out.
The pub yard's cold, wet asphalt underfoot.

From the lit shed, each answering his cue –
Gesture or rhyme – the actors come in view.

On this one evening of the mummers' play
They are no longer men of every day –

Tradition-honoured costumes clothe them all:
The wife's a young man in a wig and shawl;

Then there's St George, the Soldier, the fierce Turk
And the crab-like, black-gaitered doctor-quack,

Top-hatted, necklaced with a stethoscope,
Who, though he's sinister, gives dead men hope,

Magicks to life a trio of the slain.
Upright, at once they're fit to fight again

And in their turn give aid, restore to life
The fallen horse belonging to the wife.

This animal must be her dearest treasure –
A mount for market days or summer leisure,

So spirited, such sprightliness of tread!
His flirty tail and proudly tossing head

Seem to proclaim a noble pedigree
Although as far as anyone can see

His coat is made of ordinary sacking
And both of his front limbs are clearly lacking –

He hops on one pegleg – a walking-stick –
But he has two hind legs with which to kick

(Though gentleness can mostly be relied on),
A broad, unsaddled hessian back to ride on,

And the most wide, perceptive, saucy eyes
By turns enquiring, mischievous, or wise.

He scans the audience, ambles round unridden,
Hints with a nod at secrets best left hidden.

Even the innocent stand ill at ease
Afraid he might accuse with knowing gaze.

But he's a playful horse, not ill-intended.
Sad for him that, this evening's revels ended

Out of the limelight for twelve months he'll lie
In some dark cupboard carefully laid by,

A disembodied head in wide-eyed doze.
Who carved and painted him? Nobody knows.

Washing

Winter flays the face
flails at hands and ankles
worries away at clothing –
though wear enough layers
and it won't gnaw through.
But I've stepped heedlessly out
from the kitchen's heat.
In an instant the silk of my shirt
is a flexible steely foil loosely
encasing a fugitive layer of warmth
against skin touchy with static.

I peg up a towel, a tablecloth.
They freeze to the line,
board-stiff. No matter –
ice, no less than its liquid self,
evaporates in dry air –
though not completely in as few hours
as this dim January day affords.

At dusk I'll bring in my linen
flat and firm as builder's plywood,
watch the starchy shapes collapse,
the cloth regain its nature – pliable,
de-iced; still too wet to iron.

The Cleaning Job

She never sees a death
in the killing-place, only
death's tokens – an eyeball,
the rag-end of an ear,
body-tissue swiped
on wall and floor;
blood, shit, hair.

She'd expected
to be hoovering office carpets,
emptying waste baskets
with no worse surprises
than crusts and apple-cores,
used gum or soggy teabags.
She'd thought of dusters
and furniture polish,
of windowsills and desks.
That wasn't the way of it.

Rubber-gauntleted to the armpits,
white-clothed from crown
to booted feet, she wields
a jet of steam, swilling away
morsels and shreds of sticky dross.
Tides of raw soup, crimson and brown
white-flecked with spills of bone,
swirl into thirsty sluices,
unspeakable underfloor reservoirs.
Lips clamped until they ache,
she wills her stomach
to near-steadiness.

Four hours past midnight;
every surface starkly ready,
knives and hooks shining.
She walks away, across the cold
corral of concrete. All day
the trucks will bring heat
and noise and fear.

Dog with Snake

(on a charcoal drawing by Anne Christie)

Raised on Rikki-tikki-tavi and the lore
of snake-entrapment (allow no chance
of a strike; grasp with lightning hand
or pin down deftly in the fork of a stick
close to the swell of the head) I wonder
whether or not its zigzag stripes
declare it innocent of venom;
and if this is the dog's first snake.

Held mid-ships in clamped
half-greyhound jaws it writhes
at either end, limning arcs onto air,
never ungraceful, caught here
in a moment of switchback curves.
And no less fluid are the lines
of the she-dog's potent haunches,
her elegant spine.

This is an instant of a summer day,
outcome unknown. The snake is strong
between the vice of teeth;
can it loop round, pump poison?
The captor prances across the page.
Each is determined not to tire –
both mythical, heraldic creatures.
The slender dog. The serpent.

Dog with Tulips

A quiff of blossom (sunny jasmine,
broom?) swings beyond the pane
of the blue-painted door.

Set on a stippled cloth the tulips
lift from their coarse clay jug,
no longer pursed and private
but open-throated; saffron, syrup-gold.

Nelson, wreathed in plaited cane,
legs resting limp as string but head
raised to attention, looks towards
this late-Spring feast of colour –
appreciative you'd think.
But we are told dogs' eyes perceive
no more than shades of grey.

What of his narrow nose?
Perhaps it can comprehend
the frequencies of flowers,
savour each separate brilliance,
the scent of full-blown tulip
dazzling as any colour seen.

Keld

I half expect the Amish to come rolling onto the road
in a high-wheeled buggy, black-clothed, austere
stove-piped heads inclining neither left nor right

but every door stays shut, though it's June,
a burning day with only the lightest of breezes
and a sky where small cirrus melts as you watch.

One or two upper windows are cautiously open,
top sashes lowered by a bare handspan. No shape
or shadow is seen within; no curtain moves.

It's Sunday, the day when the cars come gleaming
between the houses to park by the inmost terrace,
nosing the line of gated hedges; the day

when a painted board leans on the barn wall –
Teas. Ice cream. Under a small-leaved sycamore,
its gentle sway answering the eddies of warm wind

a family sips and licks. In shorts and weighty boots
they're ready for a ramble on the fells.
From a nearby cottage two winter-hatted women step

into the heat. Busts heavily sweatered, hips girded
in dun-coloured tweed, they stride, eyes forward,
along the canted street.

A Hand of Musa Sapientum

A long haul home from Sydney;
just a two-hour fuelling stop
at the nadir of the night.

Among their glitzy wares
pallid young girls struggle
to stay awake. Some lie cushioned
behind the counter until at an approach
they uncurl themselves, and smile,
brown eyes effortfully focusing.

On the flight out we'd gathered
Thai silks and sequin-crusted
mantelshelf elephants, trunks
either lowered or mutely trumpeting,
and would spend now only to be rid
of the last bhats in our purses.

A coffee, because it's there, then back
to weary promenading under high stark lamps.
A crammed shop sells fruit, confectionery.
I buy seven big bananas, flawlessly yellow,
brought to their native flavour
by a full term in sunshine.

One already eaten, I'm back in the plane,
vowing restraint; but why deny myself
an airborne banquet of this food of sages?
Because greed's usually unwise
I muse, above dark interminable Russia,
to the engines' lullaby drone.

Ten Minutes in Troodos

(December)

Beyond the last lemon groves
are plots of skeletal black vines,
their few wafery leaves a dull copper –
timid first note in the mountains'
earth-drawn palette.

We climb out of the morning's cold mist
into a shock of colour. Far heights
stand sharp-cut against air-spun blue.
The road's cleft rocks gleam marble white,
mineral green, dense ox-blood red.
Strewn stones glint like malachite;
runs of rubble lie against sandy banks
loosened by last night's snow, melted now
except on shadowed slopes.

Far down, a river glistens between beaches
of bleached pebbles; poplars lift silver
and chrome-yellow quills. Every tree and bush
resolves its own autumn – all the ambers
(the cool northern, the sweet-sherry Asian),
and oddly spring-like chrysolite and beryl –
until veined leaves cede to needles.

Then the high village, winter-dressed. Ice fringes
hang arm-long from eaves above shuttered windows.
The children's playground's purely blanketed.
White chairs outside the café are plump-lapped
with whiter pads of snow. Two hound-like dogs
limp by fastidiously. That's all.
We have to leave; a meander of gentle flakes
has begun to lace the air.

Oranges and Lemons

(Cyprus, December)

We walked between long ranks
of tall trees crowded close, each veiled
from crown to ground, secluded
within a density of leaf on leaf.
Against the glossy greenness
yellow-gold and fire-gold baubles
shone in the sun – generous gifts
pinned to the dark robes.

Yesterday, windfalls were few.
This morning I wonder how many
will crowd the grass, snatched down
by the raucous gusts that since last night
have harried the island and its seas.
Out to the horizon white curling crests
gleam upon sunlit ultramarine;
beachside flags stream from their poles,
starch-stiff against an innocent sky,
cloudless, baby-ribbon blue.

December weather can change in a moment,
breezes now kind, now bitter, sheeting rain
suddenly dowsing the trees' shine;
yet through these winter moods the fruit ripens,
ready for wooden crates and distant markets.

Peeling a Pomegranate

Ovary packed with seminal trees,
it fits to the palm; an orb
still crowned with copper sepals
cupping a fusty residue of stamens;
and sometimes even the pistil remains –
the sprig of a fine sewing-needle
left in the work, warped and rusty.

Try to peel it. It's cased tight
in a rind like old leather, the surface
stained ruby and buff, slurred with black,
lightly lacquered and hard when you tap it
(that's only a bold face; the pith
beneath is porous as worn shammy).
You dig with your fingernails
but one small flake at a time
is the most that comes away.

Best to cut across its equator with a sharp knife,
slicing through kernelled jewels – they'll ooze
thin pink blood. Prise them out until you see
the pattern coming clear. Not, as it seemed
to me in childhood, a random maze
but chambers enclosed, though unevenly,
by eight walls to which the glistening fruits
are held in clusters shrink-wrapped
in translucent yellow membrane.

To have made these discoveries
you'll have been eating as you go,
crunching on seeds, experiencing
small irony-sweet explosions on the tongue –
the desert-traveller's tiny purse of drink.
Your fingers and palms drip juice.
You need to rinse your hands.

Bondi

When we were lovers
we walked on Hampstead Heath –
the city a distant sea, St Paul's afloat.
Is this all? he said...

Now I stand on the beach he talked of.
A group of life-guards dare the surf,
broad-chested, young, as he'd been then,
smooth bodies brown and oiled.

I take my sandals off and for the first time
feel the cool touch of the Pacific,
a ritual moment.
Then someone calls. The coachdriver

revs his engine; the exhaust expels
a vaporous mirage. I try to hurry
but the sand is so fine, shifting and difficult.
Thirty people watch impatiently

and can't know I'm struggling
with more than the sloping beach.
I have come round the world for this –
this ordinary Australian playground –

and he not here, nor anywhere.

Arcimboldo in Venice

Masks crammed into small-shop windows,
gilded, enamelled, baleful or virginal, peer
empty-eyed at streets where everyday Venetians,
with their long-jawed, un-Italian faces,

go about their business, while we wander,
savour – lie supine for Titian's ceiling episodes
of biblical murder, ponder Ernst's conundrums,
then follow insistent bridgeside banners

to arrive at spacious rooms, a gallery
where flesh is vegetable, flushed by juice
not blood – a wealth of greengrocery
clustered in seasonal portraiture.

Apples, grapes, onions, pears and figs,
carrots and peaches, arranged for shape
and character, present a parody
sustained on canvas after canvas.

Is this the way he saw, some quirk
of eye or mind? Or did he mean to stress
mortality, the ancient truth that men,
however great they grow, are just elaborate grass...

Poppies near Argenteuil

(Claude Monet)

How buoyantly these red blooms ride
the meadow's slope, a stilled flotilla,
the more vivid on a day
that lacks the fullest splendour
of impressionist light.

A gleam of sunshine brightens
the field's far edge, but the woman
in the foreground lowers her parasol,
as she stands beside her child
who's holding poppies.
Or perhaps they're moving forward,
slowly, through the parched grass,
a haze of seed-plumes
dense to her waist-height,
hardly a ripple troubling
the lush soft wash.

These two set in the hay's plenty,
their creamy hats small echoes
of the creamy clouds, would soon
be gone but that the painter holds them
here in an unmown pasture
that, it seems, might stay for ever
calm and warm. The poppies
tell only of peaceful living
and high summer.

The Flotation Tank

Five months now I've been driving
daylong, taking any runner primed with fuel,
but nowhere finding what I need, a living
man, live seed. The roads are still,
nothing to move or breathe but wind
and insects, winged or crawling –
except by the seashore, where I found
limpets and crabs, but no gulls calling;
and no fish stranded, so perhaps they swim
salt-safe, as I was in the closed
dark chamber's buoyant dream.
All the world's shell-less flesh is dust
except, it seems, for me and – useless gold –
the unkindled lives I hold.

Afloat

One summer from the deck
of a derelict sailing barge
its salted black hull fast
on a river sandbank

I watched a shoal of jellyfish
float by on the outward tide
flower-like and silent sliding
towards the estuary

choicelessly riding out
as they'd ridden in
on the salty flow
their one life-medium.

This evening, coloured forms
lift across pale sky
carried on cooling currents
the drift of air-streams.

Announced by sighs
their sudden spurts of flame
enhancing buoyancy
they clear the city rooftops

and we gaze up delighted
by their bright silks glossy
in near-sunset light and by
the eccentricity of the endeavour.

Sand

whispers around the world; rides
its currents in cloudy shoals of motes
ground so small that single colours,
shell or mineral, coalesce
in parched or shoreline sweeps of yellow,
rusty orange, silver-white;

above high-water, without moisture's hold,
runs to embrace the foot – each step
a trudging push and lift, each impress
shortlived in the dinted mottle
always in flux, unless night-sealed
by a cool varnishing of dew or mist;

dune-piled, slides gently grain by grain
from swell to dip, or flies loose,
wind-spun from crest and ridge; rebuilds
against stems of marram grass and sea holly;
leans along seafront walls; skims
across promenade pavements;

glutted at the ebb is sea-margin terra firma –
supports striding workboots, the loll
of beached boats; endures tractor tyres,
the strike of cantering hooves;
can be spade-cut or moulded
to shortlived steadfastness;

is the depth and breadth and barrenness
of desert, vast shapes of ripple and wave
set primevally you'd think, but sand
escapes from form to form, is drawn
from light to secrecy to light,
can take a body deep into itself,

hold it – not plumply, as ice may,
but sucked to leathered bone;
has dry-drowned and kept from sight
evidence, histories; has stifled
whole cities with its weight;
does not bloom or fruit or fester;
is not the stuff of life.

Preston

(on a painting by Dame Laura Knight)

Three hours to kill on a cold day
in an unfamiliar city. Think of ways
to keep warm, use the time.
I trudge the market's chilling stones,
eat a warm lunch, at last
find the museum.

Years ago I came home from New York
not having seen all that I might have;
some pleasures saved for next time.
It's the same on any visit, a cache
salted away, the future's hostage.

But from each gallery I save a little –
mind-slides I don't thereafter lose.
At Newcastle murky dockside views;
at York, T.S. Cooper with more sheep than cows,
at Liverpool a hundred coloured jugs
and now at Preston, fresh as yesterday,
a group of WAAFs repairing a balloon,
the ground spread with silken silver –
lustre transcending paint.

Rooster

Sunshine enhances him.
His brass, gold, copper, steel and jet
bloom to a shifting sheen. His crest
is blood-red ruching gathered posy-style
to crown the pea-brain head. His gaze
is to either side; one amber target-eye,
shiny as glass, surveys me steadily.

As if embarrassed (like a cat that suddenly
begins to groom its fur), he stoops to whet
his shrewd beak on a cobblestone;
then flounces his layered shouldercloak,
flaps flightless wings to cool his sides
and strolls off to settle in the shade.

He knows I'm watching, comes again
to stand before me, sideways on –
weathervane prototype, high fore and aft
like a sea-going wooden ship, all silent splendour
until, stretching to utmost height,
he racks himself to make his raucous call,
cockadoodle doo
at least a dozen times.

His hens remain indifferent.
For a moment, eyeing the speckled one,
he clearly contemplates a pounce;
but it's not worth the effort – he's away,
pacing the breadth of his life's kingdom,
the buttercupped and daisied lawn.

Sericulture

First you collect the eggs you call silkseed.
You keep them neither too warm nor too cold
until, when tender mulberry buds unfold,
black pinhead worms emerge, begin to feed.
When they've grown pale and fat and finger-long
they arch themselves, in unison begin
to wind their shrouds – though what they mean to spin
is shelter; a safe privacy their strong
cradles of tight-spooled filaments should provide
until, slow processes of change complete,
they hatch anew, winged creatures now, to flourish
in airy freedom. That's what should betide,
but silk ensnares the worm in grievous fate –
to gnaw and spin, and then, in limbo, perish.

Three Ways to a Silk Shirt

You have to kill for silk
and it's not easy. Those chrysalides
make themselves so private
in their tight shuttles, so safe
that they can dare to lose themselves
to metamorphosis, abandon the known body
and endure who can imagine what liquidity
before another form takes shape.

They must be murdered in the midst
of miracle, their cerements reeled off,
the long continuous thread saved
pliable, unstained, the severing bite
of the emerging moth forestalled.

The method's suffocation –
the oldest way by baking in hot sun;
but this hardens the thread,
makes unwinding a hard labour,
risks soiling by windborne dust,
is wasteful.

Steaming's another way – the plump bolls held
above a boiling cauldron for eight minutes
then for eight weeks spread out to dry
well-aired, so that the corpse in the shroud
desiccates slowly, leaves no stain;
but sometimes the chrysalis survives.

Surest is heated air. A single day exposed
to the technology of fans and ducts, the flow
of arid currents, and the pupa's void,
a juiceless chitin spindle shrivelled back
from the close wrappings drawn and spun
out of its former self – now to be unwound
and spun again: woven, dyed, cut and sewn,
collared and cuffed.

The Best Place

The paint's white as it left the brush
though soap and elbowgrease
have somewhat dulled its gloss.

No dust rests on the sills
or drifts to lie by door-jambs
or ravels into felty skeins

beneath uncluttered beds.
Here meals are served thrice
daily, eaten in unison. Plates

whisked through a hot sluice,
are pristine for re-use.
Clothes are made spruce,

purged of old smears and stains
though shrunk a bit and harsh
to the skin from the mass

washtub, the final toss
in hot tumbled air. Chairs
in the dining room are set in fours

but in the lounge there's space
to sit in a wide circle, rest
on firm high-cushioned seats –

the thrones of age, tall backs
smooth wooden arms. Upstairs
duvets are chaste as clouds

and there's a bell to press
if the small hours bring fears
or faintness – night-duty ears

are listening, and the voice
that answers knows how best
to comfort; it's all in the price.

Here patient helpers
strive to outwit nature – spills
sopped up in a trice.

All is plastic-daisy fresh,
convenient, unembellished;
panelled doors made flush

brown-mottled floors
matt-polished, no one slips
on rugs or shiny steps.

Outside are tidy lawns
and flowerbeds, and seats
for warm and windless days,

and stoneless pathways
where the frail may pace.
In this place all renounce

solitude, singleness
and live by rules
like nuns or prisoners

except that these
have neither taken vows
nor sue to be released.

After V.E. Day

The flight was a reward, a day-long jaunt,
for two of us from Met – Mae Wests, a pack
of rations. Not a tour, we thought, to daunt
or horrify – our crew were journeying back
through memories of flak and probing light,
of danger's height, the kite a glistening moth;
then, lucky, bombs away. But on this flight
they'd neither deal, nor fear to suffer, death.

I settled in the nose, a perspex curve,
sunlit blue sea beneath, clear blue around.
By Holland's fields our steady shadow moved,
then over razed towns, wastes of rubbled ground.
Victors, we'd come to witness and rejoice.
All I could think was *I've been part of this.*

Blank Verse

Between my leaving school and leaving home
(her home, my childhood home) the habit grew –
a blank verse dialogue. To be or not
to be might have been better stuff, but ours
was off the cuff, extempore – unpenned
pentameters. Iambic feet, it's said,
best suit the cadences of English speech.
Our talk seemed proof; the rhythm would catch our tongues
even at breakfast.

'How's your grapefruit, dear?'

'It's fine. I wonder if there's any post...'

'I'll go and see. But watch your egg meanwhile.
The sand's half through and you don't like hardboiled.'

'Were there some letters?'

'Just a magazine.'

'I shan't be home until quite late tonight.
There's a good film on at the Everyman.
Enfants du Paradis. I'm going with Steve
straight after work.'

'I'll save some supper.'

'Thanks.
Good heavens – can that really be the time?
I'll have to run to make it for half-past.
Bye, love...'

I wasn't there at her last breath
to wish her flights of angels and sweet rest.
My brother held her hand until she slipped
beyond iambics into verseless death.
Our long play's done and I've no heart to write
a couplet, tritely rhymed, to mark its end.

Partners

From our journeys we'd return to the usual questions;
but *No*, we'd say austerely, *we didn't expect to enjoy ourselves.*
No time for theatres or slow dining.
We'd trudge round trade shows, rest swollen feet at evening.
Meals self-sevice kept us going.

There should have been more moments of shared idleness,
more hours free of the harness we made for ourselves.
I think with compassion of the harvest horses of my childhood
leaning their heads together as they stood in the stubbled field,
each encouraged and comforted by the odour of the other's sweat.

Parallels

The cadaver dominates the painting –
flaccid flesh, a terrible pallor.
One of the figures, kneeling,
supports the rag-wrapped shoulders.
How many years since I saw that image?
The place, the painter's name, forgotten;
but my mind's eye resurrects
the crowd's robes, old blues and reds,
the propped torso, limp legs
thigh to thigh, ankle to ankle.

Was it Christ lifted down,
or Lazarus risen?
Leaning against pillows
I contemplate the bedclothes moulded
to a long mound that narrows
towards my comfortable feet.

Ladders, and Snakes

What a state it's in –
a scuffed old board
scribbled with comments.
Should have... Why didn't...?

The snakes are there, but the die
has a will of its own, always falls
so that you miss the serpent's head,
are never sent sliding back.

On you must go, towards
the top corner, slowly
square by square, or swiftly
skimming the rungs. The ladders

of course are shorter near the end,
and without the intervention
of snakes the game goes quickly.
Strange that I used to hate

the great python undulating down
from almost goal to almost start.

Chase

I saw how she started the dream,
pursued it; knew, or thought I knew,
she would run it to earth, then
almost gladly hold back
and give it space.

It was a mythic quarry,
flashing through copses, pausing
to tantalise in gateways,
making a game of the quest
she'd so earnestly begun.

She should not mourn for the loss
of that unbroken creature.
White phantoms, golden saddles,
come at a price
and are not for riding.

Incubus

How soon it's shown its will!
Nausea is my twenty-four-hour companion;
no glut of rich dessert or lavish fry-up
has ever caused such pitch of queasiness.
And while I soon lose whatever food
I try to swallow, the imp in my womb
goes on relentlessly nourishing itself.

How can I not resent the loss
of autonomy and strength, resent
the selfishness of this incubus – made,
ironically, of our generosities?
We've been sufficient to each other,
a pair of matched birds soaring
like those on the willow-pattern plate
or so it seems now – our wings clipped,
the halcyon days of pairship over.

And what's come over you, man, who's always
sung hymns to childlessness?
Suddenly you're glazed with pride,
solicitous. More evidence of the thing's
sly purposes, my loosening hold.

The Woman in the Teashop Said

I'm leaving my brain to medicine.
She had a cheerful face, lively eyes,
her skin's smoothness scarcely touched
except by delicate lines that deepened
as she smiled.

Her brain had willed its future –
not to be buried or burned in its lifelong cradle
but severed at the stem and studied
like a compact universe
where life once flourished.

Was it a humdrum brain she offered,
or in the league of laureates?
And is that of any consequence,
the precious stuff simply a moulded shape
once the current fails...

The woman in the teashop surely accepts
her death's reality. I can't imagine mine,
the cancellation, the reduction to cold trash,
the senses blanked off – even that mercy
not quite credible.

The Victorians feared burial alive,
exacted promises of a mirror to the lips;
but breath may be resumed, restored,
the heart shocked to re-start. The sole
criterion of death is now the brain's quietus,

heralded, it seems, by a final salvo,
minuscule bursts of energy, perhaps random
or perhaps to an imprinted scenario
of virtual-reality welcome, a pleasurable
passage, a beckoning fullness of light.

There's comfort in the thought of brief euphoria
then absolution from endless time.
A pensive silence followed
the teashop declaration – our brains
trying to make up their minds.

Honoured by Seraphim

It's afternoon. I rest on my bed, eyes closed,
and know they are there, one on either hand
turned towards each other – motionless, benign,
incorporeal; and vast.

They're sculptured from nothing that's material
yet I sense their substance, at once opaque and lucent.
They shine without light, screened gently
by their garments' hueless folds.

The room can hold only the lower fall
of the height they reach, lofty columnar beings
rising unhindered through my ceiling
and beyond all the storeys of this tall house

to an unguessable eminence. Enough, to receive
the smallest part of their composure.
I can ask them nothing, not even why they come
to this bed, this unbeliever.

We Had the Stars

Erotic, yet purely white, twin cigarettes
between his lips were lit by a single flame.
One was for her to smoke, a kiss
made manifest, toyed with, puffed at

with head tilted back, eyes half-closed.
Such sacramental intimacy! A ploy
for any would-be sophisticate to practise
over a couple of gin and limes with ice.

The more-than-life-size romances
of monochrome coloured our lives,
showed us myths of fulfilment
or, more potently, of sacrifice.

Violins and an ooze of slow tears
would cue cameras to blur the focus,
soften coiffed hair to a near-halo
as the bitter end approached.

God Save the King.
The seats clapped back to vertical.
We bunched out onto suburban pavements,
satisfied, purged.

Watching those vintage films on television
is like coming across dry perfume bottles,
sniffing their vagueness, wanting again
that irrecoverable tang.

Afterword, 1998

Just after midnight.
Courtesy of Sony and Channel 4.
Titles that need subtitles.
Ferocious rain, the shelter of a ruin.
The tales begin.

A glide in sunlight
above canopies of leaves,
down to a bushy glade;
a woman's hat, round as a full moon,
caught on a thorn.
From undergrowth two naked arms
reach up in rigor, fingers clawed.
The witness flees in fear.

A couple and a horse halt on an open path.
Approaching without threat a renegade
pretends goodwill, tempts with the promise
of shared treasure. The woman's beautiful –
he's fired at first by lust,
not bent on murder.

But the husband's fate is death,
trussed in his robes of caste.
The wife, immaculate chattel,
will be thrown down, disarrayed.
Dishonoured willingly, the robber boasts,
swaggering towards sentence.

That's the bare bones of the tale,
fleshed three ways in the telling;
a fourth, my own recall, proves now
to have been false from the first frame.
Memory, it seems, made its singular way
through the stories' maze, preserved
a set of stills that, though discredited,
stay in the mind, icons I believed in.